Life Transformation:

A Monthly Devotional on
Romans 12:9-21

Allowing the Bible to speak to our lives today!

- Overcoming Anxiety: Finding Peace, Discovering God
- Reaching Beyond Mediocrity: Being an Overcomer
- The Life Core: Discovering the Heart of Great Training
- The Godly Man: When God Touches a Man's Life
- Redemption Through the Scriptures
- Godly Beginnings for the Family
- Principles and Practices of Biblical Parenting
- Building a Great Marriage
- Christian Premarital Counseling Manual for Counselors
- Relational Discipleship: Cross Training
- Running the Race: Overcoming Lusts
- Genesis: The Book of Foundations
- Book of Romans: The Living Commentary
- Book of Romans: Bible Studies
- Book of Ephesians: Bible Studies
- Life Transformation: A Monthly Devotional
- Walking with Jesus: Abiding in Christ
- Inductive Bible Studies in Titus
- 1 Peter Bible Study Questions: Living in a Fallen World.
- Take Your Next Step into Ministry
- Training Leaders for Ministry
- Study Guide for Jonah: Understanding God's Heart

  Check out these and other valuable resources like our digital online libraries at www.foundationsforfreedom.net

Life Transformation:

A Monthly Devotional on Romans 12:9-21

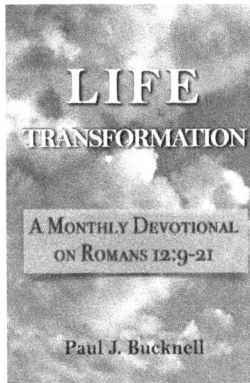

Paul J. Bucknell

Life Transformation: A Monthly Devotional on Romans 12:9-21

Copyright ©2015 Paul J. Bucknell

Printed paperback:

ISBN-10: 1619930412

ISBN-13: 978-1-61993-041-4

Also Digital e-book

ISBN-10: 1619930420

ISBN-13: 978-1-61993-042-1

www.foundationsforfreedom.net

Pittsburgh, PA 15212 USA

The NASB version is used unless otherwise stated.
New American Standard Bible ©1960, 1995 used by permission,
Lockman Foundation www.lockman.org.

Dedication

Thanks to God for sacrificing His only Son Jesus Christ to call us to assemble in His presence and be His people forever. What a joy to know each other, be mutually encouraged, and have opportunity to serve Him together forever in His love. All the hard labors we now endure will become our old 'war stories' that we will share with each other once we reach home beyond heaven's shores. The Lord purposes to forever share His joy with us as His family.

> *"What we have seen and heard we proclaim to you also, that you also may have fellowship with us; and indeed our fellowship is with the Father, and with His Son Jesus Christ. And these things we write, so that our joy may be made complete"* (1 John 1:3-4).

Table of Contents

Preface

God, with great care and design, transforms His people to increasingly reflect Christ's likeness. Sometimes we are growing and excited about our Christian growth, but at other times, our dull spirits are well-served by a fresh look at spiritual truths so that God's excellent holiness might further be formed in us. These 25 terse but pointed exhortations from Romans 12:9-21 serve as a wonderful monthly devotional guide serving this purpose – one per day!

On day 1, Romans 12:1-2 is used to introduce Paul's challenge to "be transformed by the renewing of your mind." Truthfully, simple obedience radically improves our lives – may we never forget this. What usually happens, though, is that we only obey these truths when they remain at the front of our minds. When distracted with other things, the etchings of His truth that once guided our minds fade away. We soon return back to our old habits (Mt 13:22).

Paul, however, is teaching how "renewing of the minds" brings lasting changes to our lives through His Word. These deep changes in our souls take place when by God's Word we identify and resolve to have these truths supplant our old responses, values and beliefs. Below each of these exhortations, hidden from our sight, resides a set of values and assumptions that support that truth. For more permanent positive change to take place we must be challenged at this fundamental level.

This study guide will help you prayerfully meditate on these instructions so that these deeper transformation points take place. As we reevaluate our thoughts and values, a deeper commitment combined with clear guidance will lead us into a fuller Christian life. Transformation of the mind occurs when, quietly before the Lord, we allow the Holy Spirit to implant God's deeper values into our own deeper life assumptions. Instead of temporary help, we gain a renewed approach to living out our lives – resulting in life transformation to God's glory.

An Introduction

This book largely consists of the 30 daily devotionals. Their description is below. We have a larger purpose, however. We use these devotionals to train His people how God renews a believer's mind. At some point, read appendix 1 where this whole process of how God renews our minds by His truth is taught, thus enriching our pursuit of life transformation. Another appendix offers a link to a video where one can watch a class on this important subject, while yet another appendix holds my personal testimony.

After focusing on Romans 12:2 for the first day where our 'life transformation' is sourced and discussed, we immediately jump into Paul's 25 exhortations, one for each day – all from the later part of Romans 12. The devotional studies purposely share the same structure so that one can easily focus on the studies. Since this is a month's worth of devotionals, a few extra days to review and expand this theme of transformation are appended at the end, making a total of 30.

Each study has four distinct parts, enabling us to take each exhortation and allow it to penetrate our own practices, thoughts and assumptions (see appendix 1 on how this works). Don't worry about getting stuck as each study has its own analysis, questions and even a sample prayer to get you started. Of course, we feel this monthly guide is just a beginning of developing the habit of allowing you to regularly have God's Word renew your minds.

Part #1: Biblical meditation

The brief exhortations are easily memorized, allowing us to personally encounter the significance of the phrase. Ask, "What does it mean?" "Do I already obey this or not?"

Part #2: Personal reflections

Having allowed the scripture to enter our minds, we often discover places of resistance to full compliance of God's truth. This resistance identifies our 'objections,' allowing us to more deeply understand our doubt that hinders us from embracing God's command. One objection is given as an example but room is given for you to write down the relevant objections that you have, at one time or another, used.

Part #3: Penetrating deeper

This third section provides a paragraph allowing us to better grasp the verse's meaning and implication for our lives. The brief analysis enables us to understand key definitions and other significant elements affecting our interpretation and application of this instruction.

Part #4: Relevant prayer

These brief sample prayers help put the right words in our mouths, leading us to the needed exploration, confession and thanks before God. They are designed to take us beyond superficiality into a close and intimate relationship with God. During renewal of our minds we adopt biblical perspectives, find forgiveness and freedom from false thoughts and practices, and commit ourselves to an ongoing pursuit of God who guides us through the application of these truths.

The prayers are meant to speak aloud from the heart. By all means adjust the words to better fit your particular situation. Be honest. They are not the 'expert' prayers but a tool to help everyone gain the most from these studies. By the month's end, you should see what a good prayer is and regularly form your own prayers rising from your reading of God's Word. Some will not need these written prayers; that is fine. Say your own prayer but make it personal and reflective of the teachings in the verse.

Day #1: Transformation

- *And do not be conformed to this world, but be transformed by the renewing of your mind.... (Ro 12:2)*

Biblical meditation

- Memorize the above verse until you can slowly say it three times without a mistake.
- Ask yourself, "How much of my mind has been transformed?" Write your reflections to this question below.

Personal reflections

- Jot down any objections to obeying this truth. (Sample provided below.)

  Objection: Can I really improve the way my mind thinks?

  Objection:

  Objection:

- From your above observations write down what you doubt about this truth. How has your perspective (i.e. mind) grown since becoming a believer?

Penetrating deeper

God's Word purposely challenges us to transform our minds to be unlike the world (Rom 12:1) and increasingly pleasing to God. This spiritual discipline requires personal effort and focus, but it is the only way to remove our affections from the world and personally draw closer to God.

Relevant prayer   Integrating truth into your life through prayer!

Dear Lord, I have a big problem believing the world has more to offer than you. I am so sorry. Please forgive me. I see my thoughts about the world have held me back from more fully devoting myself to you. Your ways are better than anything in this world. I choose to be close to you. Help me. In Jesus' name I pray, Amen.

Day #2: Genuine

- *Let love be without hypocrisy. (Ro 12:9)*

Biblical meditation
- Memorize the verse until you can slowly say it three times without a mistake.
- Ask yourself, "Do I love people without any hypocrisy?" Write your reflections to this below.

Personal reflections
- Jot down any objections to completely obeying this truth.

  Objection: "But what if I don't really love them?"

  Objection:

  Objection:

- From your objections, observe and write down what you doubt about this truth. Why is it that you are sometimes hypocritical?

Penetrating deeper
Hypocrisy hints of a pretentious love, a willingness to present a false view of oneself to another. We are forced to ask, "Can there be genuine love with hypocrisy?" No, love supersedes one's preoccupation with self by an authentic concern for meeting the needs of others.

Relevant prayer
Dear Lord, your love is always so genuine, but not mine. I can think of instances where I faked my love. Please forgive me through Christ. I don't want a pretend 'love' but for your life-changing love to so utterly fill me that I will love others without any hypocrisy–because I genuinely care for them and want the best for them. In Jesus' name, I pray, Amen.

Day #3: Pure

* *Abhor what is evil. (Ro 12:9)*

Biblical meditation
- Memorize the verse until you can slowly say it three times without a mistake.
- Ask yourself, "Where and when do I compromise with God's holy standard here?" Write your reflections to this question below.

Personal reflections
- Jot down any objections to completely obeying this truth.

  Objection: "But then I can't watch my programs!"

  Objection:

  Objection:

- From your observations, write down what you doubt about this truth. Are you convinced evil is really bad? What makes something evil?

Penetrating deeper
This injunction to hate evil reveals that at times we live in a casual relationship with evil. 'Hate' is more than avoidance but an intense dislike for something. Hate does not allow for compromise. Our lives are protected when our heart dislikes any shade of wrong. By the Spirit's help we need to understand what evil is and how to detest it.

Relevant prayer   Integrating truth into your life through prayer!
Dear Lord, I thank you for this exhortation. I need it. I have been pretending a little wrong is okay. I was never honest enough to call and treat it as an evil that I should hate. Please forgive me. I repent from my inclination to evil. I want to be holy, Lord. In Jesus' name I pray, Amen.

Day #4: Desirous

♦ *Cling to what is good. (Ro 12:9)*

Biblical meditation

- Memorize the verse until you can slowly say it three times without a mistake.
- Ask yourself, "How tight do I hold to what is good?" Write your reflections to this question below.

Personal reflections

- Jot down any objections to completely obeying this truth.

  Objection: "But I don't have time to meet with God and have devotions."

  Objection:

  Objection:

- From your observations about your objections, write down what you doubt about this truth. What do you need to let go of so you can better grasp what is good?

Penetrating deeper

The instruction implies that we often set our hearts on evil and inferior things. 'Cling' reveals our strong grip on what we treasure. 'Good' includes all the wholesome plans, resources and relationships appointed by God for our lives. The word 'cling' demands our whole attention, requiring that we release other fetishes.

Relevant prayer

Integrating truth into your life through prayer!

Dear Lord, I can now see how I say I want to be a strong Christian but really do not mean it. I hold onto things from the world. I do not give them up and take up the cross. Please forgive me Lord for holding back my life and affections. I give those things up for the sake of knowing and serving you, my Lord. In Jesus' name I pray, Amen.

Day #5: Caring

- ◆ *Be devoted to one another in brotherly love. (Ro 12:10)*

Biblical meditation
- Memorize the verse until you can slowly say it three times without a mistake.
- Ask yourself, "Am I committed to loving others or do I hold back?" Write your reflections to this question below.

Personal reflections
- Jot down any objections to completely obeying this truth.

  Objection: "But can't I just be nice?"

  Objection:

  Objection:

- From your observations about your objections, write down what you doubt about this truth. Do you sense a real genuine concern for others or are you prodded by guilt or what others might think of you?

Penetrating deeper
This command to be devoted to loving one another provides insight into how easily we trivialize this primary command, relegating it as less important than the meeting of our own needs. Brotherly love is the kind and expected treatment of others, as if they are family members. The word 'devoted' here is more literally translated 'be kindly affectionate.' Set aside any inclination to underrate the high call to be kind to other members of Christ's body.

Relevant prayer
Dear Lord, your people are hurting because of neglect, mine included. I know you want to love others through my life but I am so busy focusing on my own needs that I certainly am not 'devoted' to serving others. Please

forgive me and refocus me on getting up to speed in serving others. In Jesus' name I pray, Amen.

Day #6: Respectful

- *Give preference to one another in honor. (Ro 12:10)*

Biblical meditation
- Memorize the verse until you can slowly say it three times without a mistake.
- Ask yourself, "How often do I change what I do because of my preference for others?" Write your reflections to this question below.

Personal reflections
- Jot down any objections to completely obeying this truth.

  Objection: "But I like to be noticed."

  Objection:

  Objection:

- From your observations about your objections, write down what you doubt about this truth. Do you really believe others should get that special treatment? Who will care for you?

Penetrating deeper
Preferring others over ourselves is linked to our attitudes toward them. 'Give preference' focuses on their needs while the word 'honor' speaks of their importance. They are important due to being called by the Lord, and therefore we must pay special attention to their wants and needs, as if they are our honored guests. As we respond to preferring those around us, our 'me' instinct will start fading away.

Relevant prayer
Integrating truth into your life through prayer!

Dear Lord, I really have a hard time preferring others. I want people to prefer me! I do and say things so people will think better of me. Please forgive me for my selfish heart. Lord, establish that genuine sense of respect for others in me that actually changes the way I think and treat them. In Jesus' name I pray, Amen.

Day #7: Tenacious

* ◆ *Not lagging behind in diligence. (Ro 12:11)*

Biblical meditation
- Memorize the verse until you can slowly say it three times without a mistake.
- Ask yourself, "Are you diligently serving others and the Lord or slacking off here and there?" Write your reflections to this question below.

Personal reflections
- Jot down any objections to completely obeying this truth.

  Objection: "But I am used to just getting by."

  Objection:

  Objection:

- From your observations about your objections, write down what you doubt about this truth. Why do you think slacking off is better?

Penetrating deeper
This warning of lagging behind in diligence hints at how people put off what is important and compromise excellence. 'Not lagging' suggests laziness or shifting of responsibilities. 'Diligence' is the persistence in doing what is right and makes up for our imperfections. The Lord's calling sets us in the path to fulfilling His 'good works' for our lives (Eph 2:10), and so we give our every moment and bit of energy to properly completing His assignments for us.

Relevant prayer
Dear Lord, thanks for this wakeup call! It seems like I am sleeping my life through and begrudging what others do or don't do rather than getting

serious about what you want for my life. Please forgive me. Wash me with the blood of Christ and if possible help me catch up on doing the good that you have called me to. In Jesus' name I pray, Amen.

Day #8: Ardent

• *Fervent in spirit. (Ro 12:11)*

Biblical meditation

• Memorize the verse until you can slowly say it three times without a mistake.
• Ask yourself, "Am I fervent in spirit?" Write your reflections to this question below.

Personal reflections

• Jot down any objections to completely obeying this truth.

Objection: "But I must not get carried away!"

Objection:

Objection:

• From your observations about your objections, write down what you doubt about this truth. Do you hear people talk negatively about those people who are extreme? Is it really so good for you to be fervent?

Penetrating deeper

This exhortation to fervency reveals how easily people can get caught up in 'just getting things done.' God is not only interested in the completion of certain tasks but in the way that they are completed. 'Fervent' is that eager and zealous push to get the tough jobs done in the right way. 'In spirit' refers not to our bodies or fists, but our inner persons and attitudes, though our bodies are influenced by this inner spirit. God's calling is a high calling and therefore requires all the energy we can muster.

Relevant prayer   Integrating truth into your life through prayer!

Dear Lord, I don't think I would consider myself fervent in spirit at all. Fervent about sports and good movies, maybe, but not about spiritual things. Forgive me for my stale heart and help me become zealous for spiritual things. The end of things is at hand. In Jesus' name I pray, Amen.

Day #9: Dutiful

* ### *Serving the Lord. (Ro 12:11)*

Biblical meditation

- Memorize the verse until you can slowly say it three times without a mistake.
- Ask yourself, "How conscious am I of serving the Lord?" Write your reflections to this question below.

Personal reflections

- Jot down any objections to completely obeying this truth.

   Objection: "But I am very busy. Where will I ever find the time?"

   Objection:

   Objection:

- From your above observations, write down what you doubt about this truth. Do you think serving the Lord is a good thing or do you begrudge Him for what you do for Him–something you **have** to do?

Penetrating deeper

This instruction to serve the Lord, though seemingly so obvious, reveals the tendency to divorce our lives from our Master's wishes. 'Serving' is that wrestling of our will to complete the desires of another, in this case, the Lord Jesus. All what we do must be connected to the greater purpose of accomplishing what our Lord desires. As His servants, everything we do should be conscious service to Him, not just to our employer, colleague, parent or youth advisor.

Relevant prayer   Integrating truth into your life through prayer!

Dear Lord, there are so many things that I am busy with that I forget your service, it is shuffled to the back burner of priorities so that it becomes ignored. Forgive me. Please grant me a renewed honor of what it means to serve you my Lord. All I do should be part of my service to you! In Jesus' name I pray, Amen.

Day #10: Expectant

- ***Rejoicing in hope. (Ro 12:12)***

Biblical meditation

- Memorize the verse until you can slowly say it three times without a mistake.
- Ask yourself, "Am I characterized by this joy in hope?" Write your reflections to this question below.

Personal reflections

- Jot down any objections to completely obeying this truth.

  Objection: "But you don't know what I'm facing!"

  Objection:

  Objection:

- From your observations about your objections, write down what you doubt about this truth. Are you focused on hope or ensnared by thinking about what cannot be done?

Penetrating deeper

This surprising exhortation to rejoice in hope shows that, at times, we dismiss hope and miss out on its brilliant joy. Hope is that vibrant anticipatory stare that keeps us pursuing God's promises and care. 'Rejoicing' is that exuberant thrill over what God is doing, even in difficult circumstances. We need the powerful plow of hope to ramrod and cast aside all our doubts so that the seeds of hope in God can be planted in our hearts to strengthen our spirit.

Relevant prayer

Dear Lord, I thank you from the bottom of my heart about your instruction to stand with my back to disappointment and face hope. You have such a glorious and miraculous way of transforming my path into something special. I need that joy. I need you. In Jesus' name I pray, Amen.

Day #11: Enduring

- *Persevering in tribulation. (Ro 12:12)*

Biblical meditation
- Memorize the verse until you can slowly say it three times without a mistake.
- Ask yourself, "Do I persevere or give up when I hit some certain kind of difficulty?" Write your reflections to this question below.

Personal reflections
- Jot down any objections to completely obeying this truth.

  Objection: "But it's my nature to give up."

  Objection:

  Objection:

- From your observations about your objections, write down what you doubt about this truth. Do you doubt that the Lord is gone or not overseeing your life when you face trouble?"

Penetrating deeper
This exhortation to persevere in tribulation suggests that extra determination to face difficulties is needed, especially when the affliction persists. 'Tribulation' includes all sorts of difficulties that we might face when we purpose to follow the Lord. 'Persevering' is that unwavering confidence to persist in doing what is good and right, despite the opposition faced. We need a surge of confidence in God's sovereign way of working through these difficult times (Ro 8:28).

Relevant prayer   Integrating truth into your life through prayer!
Dear Lord, I do okay in some areas even when it is hard on me, but other areas, especially when I get discouraged, I give up. Please forgive me. You

didn't go half way when sending your Son to die on the cross. Keep my eyes on Jesus rather than on my circumstances. Help me not forget you are still at work when things go contrary. In Jesus' name I pray, Amen.

Day #12: Intercessor

- *Devoted to prayer. (Ro 12:12)*

Biblical meditation
- Memorize the verse until you can slowly say it three times without a mistake.
- Ask yourself, "How much do I really pray? Would you be considered devoted to prayer?" Write your reflections to this question below.

Personal reflections
- Jot down any objections to completely obeying this truth.

  Objection: "But I'm just a new Christian!"

  Objection:

  Objection:

- From your observations about your objections, write down what you doubt about this truth. How much difference do you believe prayer makes?

Penetrating deeper
This call to devoted prayer discloses the poverty of our prayer lives, at times being content with religious prayers not fortified with any real faith. Prayer is that special communion with God wherein we make our praise, confessions and needs known. The word 'devoted' speaks of that powerful drive to do something (different word used from verse 10). God wants to raise our confidence in the way God uses prayer in the life of His people.

Relevant prayer
Dear Lord, it doesn't take long to examine my prayer life! It is greatly lacking. Oh, forgive me. I must not value time with you very much. I have so far to go just to catch up. Please teach me to pray and help me start by setting a regular time to pray each day. In Jesus' name I pray, Amen.

Day #13: Generous

+ *Contributing to the needs of the saints. (Ro 12:13)*

Biblical meditation

- Memorize the verse until you can slowly say it three times without a mistake.
- Ask yourself, "How much do I really give to the needs of other believers?" Write your reflections to this question below.

Personal reflections

- Jot down any objections to completely obeying this truth.

  Objection: "But I have so many bills to pay."

  Objection:

  Objection:

- From your observations, write down what you doubt about this truth. Do you find yourself wanting to give but not doing it? Why?

Penetrating deeper

This exhortation to give to the needs of God's people tell us how easy it is to forget the greater needs of those around us and our responsibility to satisfy those needs. We tend to focus on what we don't have, but the Lord has us focus on our ability to meet the needs of others. 'Needs' is a catchall word. The word 'contribution' interestingly has its root word in *koinonia* (i.e. fellowship) and becomes one place God uses the community and contributions – not just financial – to accomplish His greater purposes of building up the body of Christ.

Relevant prayer

Dear Lord, I have appreciated the times people have helped me out but, Lord, I am so slow to give to others. It is like my wallet is frozen to give to the needy. Help me to understand my unwillingness to help and start caring for those who have needs around me. In Jesus' name I pray, Amen.

Day #14: Welcoming

- *Practicing hospitality. (Ro 12:13)*

Biblical meditation
- Memorize the verse until you can slowly say it three times without a mistake.
- Ask yourself, "When was the last time I had someone over?" Write your reflections to this question below.

Personal reflections
- Jot down any objections to completely obeying this truth.

  Objection: "But my place isn't good enough."

  Objection:

  Objection:

- From your observations about your objections, write down what you doubt about this truth. Do you allow messiness or an unorganized schedule to keep you from being hospitable? What can you do about it?

Penetrating deeper
Without hotels, hospitality fulfilled a big need for the traveling saints. This directive to practice hospitality in the Bible suggests possible neglect of putting up others as they travel nearby. The word 'practicing' tells us that it is not good enough to think about how we would like to host people but actually host them. God is pleased when we go out of our way and share what we have with others, even as He has shared with us.

Relevant prayer   Integrating truth into your life through prayer!
Dear Lord, I really have appreciated the few times people have had me over. I just don't know how to get from the "I want to" to actually inviting someone over. Lord, help me to better use my home and possessions to welcome others. In Jesus' name I pray, Amen.

Day #15: Big-hearted

- **Bless those who persecute you. Bless and curse not. (Ro 12:14)**

Biblical meditation

- Memorize the verse until you can slowly say it three times without a mistake.
- Ask yourself, "Do I really 'bless' people?" Write your reflections to this question below.

Personal reflections

- Jot down any objections to completely obeying this truth.

  Objection: "But I can't stand them."

  Objection:

  Objection:

- From your observations about your objections, write down what you doubt about this truth. Do you have the faith to wish God's good blessings upon others? What about those who have hurt you?

Penetrating deeper

The action 'bless' is not the typical response to persecution! The word 'bless' is twice-used, making a clear emphasis that we only have one response. Because of our suffering pain, it must be done in faith, trusting ourselves and our loved ones to God's sovereign care. Instead of just enduring, tolerating or withholding evil words, we step out in faith 'blessing' our persecutors from which they can find life.

Relevant prayer
Integrating truth into your life through prayer!

Dear Lord, I get real upset when someone doesn't treat me right. But to go to the point of blessing those who persecute me? I really need your help to do this, Lord. I can't get close to this. Please forgive me. Instill a peaceful and gentle heart in me please. In Jesus' name I pray, Amen.

Day #16: Joyful

• *Rejoice with those who rejoice. (Ro 12:15)*

Biblical meditation
- Memorize the verse until you can slowly say it three times without a mistake.
- Ask yourself, "Do I actually get over my envy and rejoice with others?" Write your reflections to this question below.

Personal reflections
- Jot down any objections to completely obeying this truth.

  Objection: "But why should he or she get all the breaks?"

  Objection:

  Objection:

- From your observations about your objections, write down what you doubt about this truth. Can you detect any selfishness in you that repels the notion of being glad for others?

Penetrating deeper
This reminder to rejoice with others shakes us from our petty jealousies and unholy competitions. Paul awakens us from our self-seeking lives and pushes us to get caught up in the joy of others. Passive attention is quite unsatisfactory in light of the excitement we are to have for others as they see God's hand active in their lives.

Relevant prayer   Integrating truth into your life through prayer!
Dear Lord, my old flesh has a real tough time being glad for others. I so desperately want that attention that it is hard for me to be joyful for others. Please forgive me and help me to regularly delight in the blessings that others receive. In Jesus' name I pray, Amen.

Day #17: Empathetic

- ### *Weep with those who weep. (Ro 12:15)*

Biblical meditation
- Memorize the verse until you can slowly say it three times without a mistake.
- Ask yourself, "When was the last time someone went through a hard time near me. Did I 'weep' with them?" Write your reflections to this question below.

Personal reflections
- Jot down any objections to completely obeying this truth.

  Objection: "But I have enough of my own problems."

  Objection:

  Objection:

- From your observations about your objections, write down what you doubt about this truth. Are you involved in other people's lives so that you cry as they cry?

Penetrating deeper
Paul's command to weep with others again directs our attention away from ourselves and onto others, even when they go through tough times. Others might state, "Don't get involved in others so that you do not suffer with them" but this is not the mindset here. We are challenged to grieve with others because we are involved in their lives and sympathize with them.

Relevant prayer   Integrating truth into your life through prayer!
Dear Lord, I do know that caring for those who are going through a rough time is important, but, to be honest, it is so far from my experience. I rush through my life so fast that I can't even see those around me who are in need. I have a natural tendency to avoid such people. Please forgive me and help me start caring. In Jesus' name I pray, Amen.

Day #18: Unassuming

- ### *Be of the same mind toward one another. (Ro 12:16)*

Biblical meditation
- Memorize the verse until you can slowly say it three times without a mistake.
- Ask yourself, "Do I consider others as important as myself?" Write your reflections to this question below.

Personal reflections
- Jot down any objections to completely obeying this truth.

  Objection: "But I just do not get along with that person!"

  Objection:

  Objection:

- From your observations about your objections, write down what you doubt about this truth. For example, are there some people that are hard for you to get along with? What is your attitude towards them?

Penetrating deeper
This caution to guide our attitudes towards others not only keeps us from pride but brings us deeper into the bond of love. When our biases and arrogance are stripped away, we see each brother and sister as God's special design. God is shaping them into Christ's image just as He is doing with us. This faith strengthens our commitment to others.

Relevant prayer
Dear Lord, I know I should not look down on people. With most people I don't have a problem, but I just have a hard time respecting those few that are not pulling their full load. I can see I need to change. Please help me to

"have the same mind" – to value everyone in the church. In Jesus' name I pray, Amen.

Day #19: Humble

- ### *Do not be haughty in mind but associate with the lowly. (Ro 12:16)*

Biblical meditation
- Memorize the verse until you can slowly say it three times without a mistake.
- Ask yourself, "Do I look down on anyone or keep myself not associating with certain people?" Write your reflections to this question below.

Personal reflections
- Jot down any objections to completely obeying this truth.

  Objection: "But I am better than him."

  Objection:

  Objection:

- From your observations, write down what you doubt about this truth. Do you think everyone in the body of Christ is special in his or her own way?

Penetrating deeper
Pride wrongly separates us from others, causing disunity rather than a strong and healthy body life. Instead of associating with the rich, connected, and intelligent, we are called to spend time caring for the average and lowly person. The church always has those who do not fit into society as we like, but these believers are very much part of the church, deserving our full respect.

Relevant prayer   Integrating truth into your life through prayer!
Dear Lord, experience and knowledge have provided many advantages for me but these things cause me to look down on others. Please forgive me. You made everyone unique, though different. Help me never to compare myself with others but to focus on appreciating other people and serving them as appropriate. In Jesus' name I pray, Amen.

Day #20: Teachable

- ***Do not be wise in your estimation. (Ro 12:16)***

Biblical meditation
- Memorize the verse until you can slowly say it three times without a mistake.
- Ask yourself, "Do I find myself thinking about myself as being wiser than others?" Write your reflections to this question below.

Personal reflections
- Jot down any objections to completely obeying this truth.

  Objection: "But I know I can do it."

  Objection:

  Objection:

- From your observations about your objections, write down what you doubt about this truth. Give an example of when you were really grateful for another person's insight?

Penetrating deeper
This prohibition to think too much of our own opinion enables us to break down possible walls of pride that might have developed in us. By esteeming our own views, practices and thoughts, we exclude ourselves from seeking insight from God and others, which negatively affects our walk with Him. Instead, let us be quick to acknowledge our weaknesses, ignorance and needs, seeking to grow in the likeness of Christ with others.

Relevant prayer   Integrating truth into your life through prayer!
Dear Lord, sometimes I am rather impulsive in my decision making. People caution me, or hint that they have something to say but I ignore them. I don't slow down and take the input you have for me through them. Forgive me for thinking so much about myself and not properly being helped by the people around me. In Jesus' name I pray, Amen.

Day #21: Self-restrained

- *Never pay back evil for evil to anyone. (Ro 12:17)*

Biblical meditation
- Memorize the verse until you can slowly say it three times without a mistake.
- Ask yourself, "Have I ever paid back someone for a wrong they have done to me?" Write your reflections to this question below.

Personal reflections
- Jot down any objections to completely obeying this truth.

  Objection: "But I am just giving back what he deserves."

  Objection:

  Objection:

- From your observations about your objections, write down what you doubt about this truth. Do you doubt that the Lord can properly care for your needs when you are wronged?

Penetrating deeper
This exhortation to not pay back evil for evil (also 12:19) is a powerful statement interrupting our flesh's desire to do wrong to those who have hurt us. As followers of Christ, we simply refuse to go along with Satan who wants to bring more evil into the world, but instead purpose ourselves to introduce the Lord's love to those around us. We are forbidden to enter into any action or contemplation to hurt someone or get back at them.

Relevant prayer   Integrating truth into your life through prayer!
Dear Lord, I greatly appreciate this warning. I feel it is so urgent to get back at others, when in fact, I should never get back at anyone, even when they hurt me. Please give me a greater trust in the way you timely care for the situations behind the scenes. In Jesus' name I pray, Amen.

Day #22: Approving

• *Respect what is right in the sight of all men. (Ro 12:17)*

Biblical meditation
- Memorize the verse until you can slowly say it three times without a mistake.
- Ask yourself, "Do I esteem what is good and right?" Write your reflections to this question below.

Personal reflections
- Jot down any objections to completely obeying this truth.

  Objection: "But I think cutting corners for myself is okay."

  Objection:

  Objection:

- From your observations about your objections, write down what you doubt about this truth. Do you hold a lesser standard for yourself than others? In what areas?

Penetrating deeper
This instruction to respect what is right leads us to accept common God-instilled values found around the globe. People are brought up having many good values embedded into their culture's moral code. Note, however, that we are not to respect all the opinions and customs of the world but those that the Lord considers as "right." This command, however, guides us into a proper respect of all the good things people do.

Relevant prayer
Integrating truth into your life through prayer!

Dear Lord, sometimes I get so intense on what people are doing wrong that I never can see, and certainly never compliment others, the good things that they are doing. Thank you for all the right decisions people make to make this society better. Please help me more deeply respect what good they do. In Jesus' name I pray, Amen.

Day #23: Forbearing

- *As far as it depends on you, be at peace with all men.* (Ro 12:18)

Biblical meditation
- Memorize the verse until you can slowly say it three times.
- Ask yourself, "In what areas have I not gone to full lengths in making peace with others?" Write your reflections to this question below.

Personal reflections
- Jot down any objections to completely obeying this truth.

  Objection: "But I can't forgive him."

  Objection:

  Objection:

- From your observations about your objections, write down what you doubt about this truth. Is there anyone you have offended? Who? For what? Make and implement a plan to initiate peace.

Penetrating deeper
This particular instruction to be at peace with all calls us to be reconciliatory at heart. Peace is the absence of conflict, a place where the tension of opposing opinions is gone. We can sacrifice our preferences to gain this peace but never our values. Whether it be a brother, spouse or colleague, we always take steps to secure the peace that can be found, never holding back on our efforts even when others withhold their due part.

Relevant prayer
Dear Lord, in the Lord's prayer you tell us to forgive, but forgiving is not easy for me. Forgive me for not being diligent in this. You are so gracious to me. Help me to identify those I haven't forgiven and this week to follow through in fully forgiving them. In Jesus' name I pray, Amen.

Day #24: Merciful

* ***Never take your own revenge, but leave room for the wrath of God.... (Ro 12:19)***

Biblical meditation

- Memorize the verse until you can slowly say it three times.
- Ask yourself, "Have I fully released the revengeful spirit against others on my heart?" Write your reflections to this question below.

Personal reflections

- Jot down any objections to completely obeying this truth.

  Objection: "But someone has to teach him a lesson or two."

  Objection:

  Objection:

- From your observations about your objections, write down what you doubt about this truth. Do you fully trust the Lord for taking care of making everything right?

Penetrating deeper

Again, as in verse 17, we are called not to take revenge. Paul elaborates on this by speaking about God's prerogative to judge. By instructing us not to take revenge does not mean that judgment will not come but that God will in His own time handle that. Our part is to forgive, make peace, and kindly treat others. Taking revenge upsets God's way of handling judgment.

Relevant prayer
Integrating truth into your life through prayer!

Dear Lord, I have repeatedly messed up things when I have attempted to 'straighten' things out. Why should I trust my ability to rightly judge others? Forgive me for my spirit of revenge. This only can rightly be done by you. Right now, in Jesus' name, I release this person for you to take care of. Amen.

Day #25: Gracious

- *If your enemy is hungry, feed him, and if he is thirsty, give him a drink. (Ro 12:20)*

1. Approving
2. Ardent
3. Big-hearted
4. Charitable
5. Desirous
6. Dutiful
7. Empathetic
8. Enduring
9. Expectant
10. Forbearing
11. Genuine
12. Gracious
13. Humble
14. Intercessor
15. Joyful
16. Loving
17. Magnanimous
18. Merciful
19. Pure
20. Respectful
21. Self-restrained
22. Teachable
23. Tenacious
24. Unassuming
25. Welcoming

Biblical meditation

•Memorize the verse until you can slowly say it three times without a mistake.

•Ask yourself, "Do I take practical steps to help those who work against me?" Write your reflections to this question below.

Personal reflections

•Jot down any objections to completely obeying this truth.

Objection: "But I am only treating him as he treated me."

Objection:

Objection:

•From your observations about your objections, write down what you doubt about this truth. Do you believe helping out your enemy in practical ways will work a greater good because of God working behind the scenes?

Penetrating deeper

Not only are we called to be kind and withhold evil from our unkind neighbor, but we are to go out of the way to graciously help them. If they are hungry, feed them. If thirsty, give them a drink. We treat our enemy as our friend, bestowing kind acts to fulfill their needs.

Relevant prayer

Integrating truth into your life through prayer!

Dear Lord, thank you for this reminder to leave my selfish spirit behind and reach out in love to those who set themselves against me. Forgive me for not trusting you in your wise ways. Help me now to be concerned and take practical steps toward these individuals. In Jesus' name I pray, Amen.

Day #26: Magnanimous

• Do not be overcome by evil, but overcome evil with good. (Ro 12:21)

Biblical meditation

- Memorize the verse until you can slowly say it three times without a mistake.
- Ask yourself, "What two good things did I confidently do overcoming evil with good?" Write your reflections to this question below.

Personal reflections

- Jot down any objections to completely obeying this truth.

  Objection: "But I am just so upset with her/him."

  Objection:

  Objection:

- From your observations about your objections, write down what you doubt about this truth. What confidence do you have that doing good has greater power than doing evil?

Penetrating deeper

This prohibition to give into evil reminds us, that without God's grace, each of us would end up overpowered by evil. But as God's people, we have God's mighty hand leading us by equipping us to overcome the tendency to do evil by carrying out acts of goodness. What a blessing it is to be able to choose and do good!

Relevant prayer
Integrating truth into your life through prayer!

Dear Lord, thank you for working so powerfully behind the scenes that I can join you in spreading your goodness and grace to others. I sometimes, being fooled, start believing that doing evil is better than doing good, but that leaves me and the world in a worse way. Forgive me and lead me to being more like Jesus in this way. In Jesus' name I pray, Amen.

Day #27: Review

• *Identify which exhortation from the list that the Lord has recently used most in your life.*

Biblical meditation

- Review that verse in your memory.
- Seek the Lord in two ways:
    - Thank Him for strengthening you.
    - While meditating on that particular verse, Ask Him, "Is there anything else that You want concerning that verse?"

Personal reflections

- In what way did you object to that truth before?

- What kind of faith did the Lord give you to change?

- How **has your mind been transformed** so far?

Penetrating deeper

Identify two things from other scriptures:

a) Write down another scripture passage that affirms that truth.

b) A biblical example of a person who did or did not carry it out.

Relevant prayer Integrating truth into your life through prayer!

Dear Lord, I appreciate the way you work in my life to transform me into Christ's image. You have revived me. Bring me closer to you through making me more aware of your truths. Please let me be not so stubborn and resistant to what you have to say. In Jesus' name I pray, Amen.

Day #28: Life Transformation Quiz

Connect the character with the instruction (Click to print):

- *Let love be without hypocrisy. (12:9)*
- *Abhor what is evil. (12:9)*
- *Cling to what is good. (12:9)*
- *Be devoted to one another in brotherly love. (12:10)*
- *Give preference to one another in honor. (12:10)*
- *Not lagging behind in diligence. (12:11)*
- *Fervent in spirit. (12:11)*
- *Serving the Lord. (12:11)*
- *Rejoicing in hope. (12:12)*
- *Persevering in tribulation. (12:12)*
- *Devoted to prayer. (12:12)*
- *Contributing to the needs of the saints. (12:13)*
- *Practicing hospitality. (12:13)*
- *Bless those who persecute you. Bless and curse not. (12:14)*
- *Rejoice with those who rejoice. (12:15)*
- *Weep with those who weep. (12:15)*
- *Be of the same mind toward one another. (12:16)*
- *Do not be haughty in mind but associate with the lowly. (12:16)*
- *Do not be wise in your estimation. (12:16)*
- *Never pay back evil for evil to anyone. (12:17)*
- *Respect what is right in the sight of all men. (12:17)*
- *As far as it depends on you, be at peace with all men. (12:18)*
- *Never take your own revenge, but leave room for the wrath of God.... (12:19)*

- *If your enemy is hungry, feed him, and if he is thirsty, give him a drink. (12:20)*
- *Do not be overcome by evil, but overcome evil with good. (12:21)*

Circle and pray for at least two areas that you would like to grow more in.

Day #29: Renewing the Mind

In Romans 12:2 Paul has told us to renew our minds. In this next to the last day, we want to briefly turn our minds back to the process the Lord uses to change us into Jesus' image.

Remembering the process (Follow instructions in appendices 1 and 2)

To the best of your ability, summarize how a believer renews his or her mind. At the same time, review the chart in appendix 1 and relate your personal experiences while going through this book.

Refreshing one's mind

Identify the two studies that helped you grow the most. What part of the process did the Lord use to cause the most changes in you?

1.

2.

Being used of the Lord

Lastly, if someone would ask you how to renew their minds, what would you say to them? List a few points of what they could do? Share one example with them from what you have learned.

1.

2.

3.

4.

Summary

If you ever hear someone state that God is not speaking to them through the scriptures, be ready to share how He wants to transform us by the renewing our minds. Ask if they have a few moments and, if so, share with them the one or two ways God blessed you and how this process works. Seek the Lord in prayer to direct your paths regarding this assignment.

Day #30: Giving Thanks

Each of us experiences different disappointments and pain as we walk through life. We want to close this month of meditations by bringing our thanks to the Lord for the way He reveals these truths to us and enables us to be free from the evil one's grasp on our lives. With each point below, find a related Bible verse.

Remember your old self

Remember several of the foolish, evil things you used to do, either before or after you believed. Thank Him for bringing you out from those dark chambers.

Bible verse:

Remember the cross

It is at the cross where we can be totally forgiven for **all** our sins. To the best of your ability visualize Jesus' road to Calvary, His pain and death. Thank Him profusely for so kindly thinking about you, forgiving you and working in you.

Bible verse:

Remember the recent victories

Victories will always be secured through the cross, but we must go beyond the cross and to His resurrection power. Thank Him for recent steps of spiritual growth through this monthly study.

Bible verse:

Look forward to future victories

We live in hope of God's continued transformation of our lives until Jesus returns when He will fully transform us into Christ's image so that we can share His full glory. Right now, in prayer, talk to the Lord about these further steps of transformation that He will bring about here on earth. Expect great things for you and others. Make it part of your daily quiet time. Build this expectancy into your spiritual life and seek God for them.

Bible verse: *"He also predestined **to become conformed to the image of His Son**, that He might be the first-born among many brethren"* (Rom 8:29)

Appendix 1: Renewing Methodology

The method by which our minds are renewed will be explained in two parts. First, we will remind ourselves how Romans 12:2 fits into the overall scheme of renewal and, second, explain how God's truth penetrates our minds and makes those significant, long-lasting and needed changes.

A. The Transformation: Romans 12:2

"And do not be conformed to this world, but be transformed by the renewing of your mind, that you may prove what the will of God is, that which is good and acceptable and perfect."

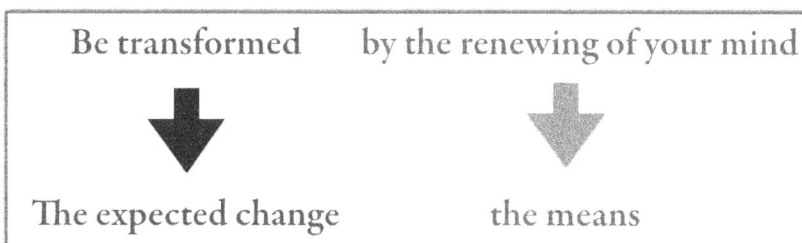

Be transformed	by the renewing of your mind
⬇	⬇
The expected change	the means

The command sets our mind on the many little steps of transformation that take place for the process of sanctification (i.e. renewing) to conform us into Christ's image. This is the clear goal ahead of us.

The process by which this transformation takes place is called the "renewing of your mind." This will be explained below.

B. The Renewing: The means

Paul here, and in other places, speaks of the important place the mind has in our spiritual development (Col 3:10-11). In the spiritual armor metaphor, several of these truths come together as part of this process: "Having girded your loins with truth," "Having put on the breastplate of righteousness," "Taking up the shield of faith," and "with all prayer and petition pray at all times in the Spirit" (Eph 6:1-18).

By reflecting on the scriptures and reflecting on the verses speaking about renewal, God has brought many of these practical changes into my own life. I share a four step renewal process noted by the following chart. Each of the four points on the chart will be explained, and an example from the list of exhortations produces further clarity.

Exhortations

Each instruction reveals weaknesses
we need to stand guard against.

e.g. "I know I should cling to
what is good; but…."

The truth is a **restatement** of what
ought to be **true** in our lives.

This is the way I
ought to be!

The exhortation challenges us to extend
our faith further in God to carry out
what He deems to be important.

Change and improvement are
difficult because of unbelief.
"I don't believe doing…."

Our resolve to obey helps us to target
the changes that we need to make in
our lives, often including a change in
our attitudes and values.

Renewing the mind
enables us to consistently
live like Jesus.

1. Targeting our weakness

The apostle's exhortations target our weaknesses, the areas we are most prone to be affected. Because of this, we should meditate on each area Paul targets to make sure that we have not been infected by the world's ways. When Paul tells us to "cling to what is good," he is at the same time inferring that at times we choose not to cling to what is good but bad – otherwise there is no need for the instruction. Our neglect to carry out these exhortations reveals ways that we have, often unknowingly, conformed to the world (Ro 12:1).

2. Defining the truth

Each exhortation becomes for us a goal reminding us of where we should be in our Christian lives. The instruction highlights what is normal, possible and good for all believers. If we carefully monitor our thoughts as we meditate on carrying out the instruction, we will begin to see the various objections that we make **in our minds**, somehow concluding that this truth does not, for some reason, apply to us in this or that situation.

Meditation on the exhortation, "Cling to what is good," forces me to define 'good' and what it means 'to cling.' We should ask ourselves (and this devotional provides us many of the necessary questions), "What are my objections to obeying this?" Or, "What aspect of the charge do I consider inappropriate?" Note how this leads us into examining what conclusions our minds have made.

3. Challenging our faith

These instructions, in turn, challenge our faith. Although we rarely understand our problems to stem from unbelief, they do. Our lack of conformity results from a lack of faith. With proper faith, we can do all these things.

When I am confident that the 'good' (again referring to the example) is superior to the world and worth clinging onto, this enables me to let go of the things of the world. But unbelief will interfere with obedience for though we might state over and over that we believe in God's Word, at this point we do not. Our disobedience betrays our lack of faith.

In the devotional, there is a place to write down what we doubt about the instruction. This is the place real change takes place – because it leads to discovery of hidden sin, unbelief, repentance and forgiveness at the cross. Renewal of the mind brings transformation of our lives.

4. Resolving God's purposes

The fourth step speaks of our resolve to make these lifelong changes. As our false values are identified, we can see our sin and unbelief, and, through the cross, reconcile ourselves with the Lord. Because the truth is on our mind, it touches our deep values and beliefs. We are now spiritually positioned to pray this through (Mat 5:3-4), starting with repentance, but going on to state the great value of the specific truth (e.g. God's goodness is far greater than what the world offers – Ps 84:10). Our faith is growing. At the same time, we allow the Spirit to lead us, supplanting the unbelief with belief, which in turn allows us to obey Him and affirm His grace working in us.

This is why each devotional has a written prayer. We want to make sure we pray this new commitment into our lives. The prayers might appear to be insignificant, but they train us to include certain things in our prayers so transformation takes place, freeing us to walk in the Spirit. Don't skip over them! In our sample prayer, we might confess our love for the world, release our hold on certain things (maybe a girl), admit the horror of our sin, gain forgiveness, state how God's goodness supersedes anything from the world and affirm our resolve to cling to what is good by God's wonderful grace. Please remember that the knowledge that we should confess our sins is quite different from actually confessing them and finding forgiveness. Prayer ushers us to that next step.

Future steps

This renewing methodology of the mind works great with other passages in the Bible too! It most effectively works with exhortations, laws, examples of sin, or obedience that we discover in the scriptures (rather than narratives). Ask yourself, "What am I learning here? Is there anything

I should do or not do from this scripture passage?" Having noted this, we can more easily spot the resistance (i.e. unbelief) that we have towards taking or not taking that action. In this way, this study method can regularly enrich our daily quiet times throughout our whole lives and not just in Romans 12:9-21!

Appendix 2: A Video Link

This is a video of a lesson I taught on Romans 12 during a teaching series through the Book of Romans. After introducing the context of the Romans 12:9-21 passage, I describe how renewal of the mind works. Most of the teaching reflects and expands upon the meaning of each exhortation, combining thoughts from the student's input on what objections they commonly make to excuse themselves from these exhortations.

Hope you enjoy and visit our website as a whole. The New Testament Digital Library [1] has all the Roman resources as well as the resources from other New Testament books forming a massive collection of very useful resources.

Romans 12:9-21 video: http://youtu.be/xSAa_-upiX8

Teaching Outline

A. What is the context of Romans 12:9-21?

B. Explain the basic aspects to the methodology of renewing one's mind and being transformed.

C. Pick out the three exhortations that you are most challenged by. What makes them so challenging?

---

[1] Digital resources: www.foundationsforfreedom.net/Help/Store/Intros/DLibrary-BibleNT.html

Appendix 3: A Personal Testimony

I personally have seen and am thrilled by how God has renewed my life through this process. So many spheres of my life have been totally reshaped by God's Word over the years. I was brought up in a very broken and non-Christian home (religious but not genuinely Christian). I grew up emotionally scarred. Those scars revealed how my mind had to some degree accommodated unbelief and needed reworking. The evil one, diligently working behind the scenes, convinced me that my conclusions (i.e. the thoughts of my mind) were proper. For example, I justified my hatred. He hid the fact that my emotional dysfunctionality was linked to my wrong conclusions (i.e. bitterness in this case). Once my mind accepted these improper thoughts, such as my inferiority and lack of worth, then they affected how I thought about myself and responded to others.

My mind had accepted these many distortions as normal and at a young age they greatly damaged my development. Like many youth, I too focused on fulfilling those deeper needs of my life. And as typical, my poor thinking was reflected in my sinful actions and words, resulting in yet further distortions.

At one point in my life, after I had started to daily study God's Word, God graciously led me into a life-changing study of the *Song of Solomon* where He changed my concepts towards myself according to His Word. I will not share this here as it is in my book, _Building a Great Marriage_, but this renewing process stood as the means God used to rebuild a foundation fit for a strong life and marriage.

Self-worth and marriage were just a few scars; others existed. (The list is so long!) Doubt or ignorance of God's Word continued to plague my mind in many areas, but it is the constant renewing of the mind through His Word that made such a great transformation of my life. I give open thanks to God for the power of His Word in my life and encourage everyone to go deeper into God's Word to acquire the changes He desires to bring about.

Author Introduction

Rev. Paul J. Bucknell has worked as an overseas church planter during the 1980s and pastored in America during the 1990s. God called him to establish *Biblical Foundations for Freedom* in 2000 and since then he has been actively writing, holding international Christian leadership training seminars and serving in the local church.

Paul's wide range of books on Christian life, discipleship, godly living, leadership training, marriage, parenting, anxiety, Old and New Testament and other spiritual life topics provide special insights that are blended into his many books and media-rich training resources.

Paul has been married for more than thirty-five wonderful years. With eight children and three grandchildren, Paul and his wife Linda continually see God's blessings unfold in their lives.

For more on Paul and Linda and the BFF ministry, check online at: www.foundationsforfreedom.net

www.ingramcontent.com/pod-product-compliance
Lightning Source LLC
Chambersburg PA
CBHW071738020426
42331CB00008B/2087